Spion Kop

by

H.G. Castle

with artwork by

Edward Mortelmans

ALMARK

ALMARK PUBLISHING CO. LTD, LONDON

First Published 1976.

ISBN 0 85524 251 5 (paper cover)
ISBN 0 85524 252 3 (hard cover)

Printed in Great Britain by
Chapel River Press,
Andover, Hants.
for the publishers, Almark Publishing Co. Ltd.
49 Malden Way, New Malden,
Surrey KT3 6EA, England.

CONTENTS

SOURCES

Amery, L. S. (editor), *The Times History of the War in South Africa*, vols I and II (London, 1900 and 1902).

Armstrong, H. C., *Grey steel, J. C. Smuts, a study in arrogance* (London, 1937).

Buller, General Sir Redvers, *His evidence taken before the Royal Commission on the War in South Africa* (London, 1904).

Burleigh, Bennet, *The Natal Campaign* (London, 1900).

Churchill, W. S., *London to Ladysmith via Pretoria* (London, 1900).

Doyle, A. Conan, *The Great Boer War* (London, 1900).

Maurice, Major General Sir Frederick, *History of the War in South Africa, 1899-1902*, vols I and II (London, n.d.).

Melville, Colonel C. H., *Life of General, the Right Hon. Sir Redvers Buller*, 2 vols (London, 1923).

Musgrave, G. C., *In South Africa with Buller* (London, 1900).

Pemberton, W. Baring, *Battles of the Boer War* (London, 1964).

Ransford, Oliver, *The Battle of Spion Kop* (London, 1969).

Reitz, Deneys, *Commando: a Boer Journal of the Boer War* (London, 1929).

Williams, Watkin, *Life of General Sir Charles Warren* (Oxford, 1941).

Wilson, H. W., *With the flag to Pretoria,* vols I and II (London, 1901).

Report on Royal Commission of War in South Africa.

Contemporary newspapers and magazines.

The Christiana commando on parade. A typical Boer commando, it included men of all social classes and ages from 16 to 70 (*The Graphic*).

1 A Fatal History: Footsteps to War

On 22 January 1900 the 60-year-old commander of the British Field Force in Natal, General Sir Redvers Buller, VC, telegraphed a dramatic signal: "Spion Kop is to be attacked tonight."

More than 7,000 miles away, in London, eager eyes examined large-scale maps and identified the hitherto-unknown Spion Kop as a 1,470 ft peak in the Heights of the Tugela River on the South African veldt. This formidable natural bastion was some 15 miles from Ladysmith, where General Sir George White, VC, and over 13,000 troops were trapped by the Boers.

Enthusiasm, optimism, and renewed hope greeted General Buller's signal. Success at Spion Kop would not only relieve beleagured Ladysmith. It would also bring a desperately needed victory.

The South African War (the Second Boer War) was a tragic climax to implacable enmity between the British and the Boers. From the early part of the nineteenth century the Boers, although of Dutch, Huguenot, and German stock, had been developing into a separate, independent people. The process was slow and sporadic. A single act, the British annexation of the Cape in 1814, created the nucleus of a common kinship.

To escape compulsory British nationality and other resented restrictions, thousands of Boers left the territory. The now immortal Great Trek took them across the Orange River to the high lands of the veldt and across the Vaal River, beyond the Drakensbergs and into Natal.

With the British still trying to impose citizenship on the *voortrekkers* (pioneers), Boer unity was strengthened by an unremitting struggle against the Zulus and Basutos, whose lands they were taking by penetration and conquest.

In 1842, the British drove the Boers out of Natal, which was given an ambiguous independence. In the Orange River territory the Boers, if they did not prosper, suffered fewer privations than their brethren who had trekked farther north. Enclosed in areas as remote and secret as "King Solomon's mines", these tenacious Transvaalers survived Zulu attacks, near bankruptcy, and extreme poverty. They lived off the country. Expert marksmen from the saddle, they could kill a running buck at 400 yards. Dismounted, they could stalk and hunt their prey at close quarters.

The British government ignored them and concentrated its plans for a united British-controlled South Africa on the Orange Free State settlers. But these obdurate Boers resisted until the home government, anxious for peaceful cooperation, granted independence to the new Orange Free State, in 1854.

Two years later, the Transvaalers unilaterally formed the ambitiously and presumptuously-named "South African Republic".

The discovery of diamonds at Kimberley in 1867 was to bring the two sides closer together and open a road to bloody warfare. The diamond fields, in an area adjacent to the Orange Free State and the Transvaal, were claimed by both Republics. Exploiting the disagreement, Britain annexed Basutoland in 1871. This not only deprived the Free Staters of essential grazing land but also united the two Boer factions in a common cause.

With the Germans and the Americans taking an unwelcome interest in South Africa, Britain annexed the Transvaal in 1877. But the Transvaalers were determined not to sacrifice a bitterly-won independence. The terms of the annexation were furiously rejected. Their intransigent leader, S. J. Paul Kruger, dismissed by the British, led them to a defiant, rebellious reconstitution of their Republic in 1880.

In February 1881, to the astonishment of the entire world, the Boers annihilated a British force at Majuba Hill in Natal, near the Transvaal border. In scale, a minor engagement of the First Boer War, it was then the most humiliating defeat ever inflicted on the British army. More significantly, it gave the Boers the power that comes out of a gun barrel.

Britain granted independence to the Transvaal under the Treaty of Pretoria in 1881. The wily, belligerent Kruger, who became President of the Republic in April 1883, scented weakness and indecision. He demanded a united Boer South Africa. The mob slogan "South Africa for the Afrikaners" was taken up by 80,000 Transvaalers.

Then, with the discovery of gold at Witwatersrand in 1886, South Africa and its Kimberley diamond mines became the richest place in the world.

Despite pious statements about protecting a simple way of life, Kruger knew the value of gold for the Transvaal. He knew, too, that there were fatal threats to the Republic: the British annexation of Zululand; Cecil Rhodes, who with his vast mining interests was later to become Prime Minister of Cape Colony; the activities of the Chartered British South Africa Company; and the greedy hordes of immigrant gold seekers.

As each critical year succeeded another, the British settlers also felt threatened. By 1899, with the Orange Free State and the Transvaal allies, they were secure only in Cape Colony. In the Transvaal the Boers exploited the foreigners, or *uitlanders,* who claimed to pay nine-tenths of the revenue but had scarcely any civic rights or representation. In April 1899 over 20,000 of them submitted a "humble petition" to Queen Victoria asking for protection and armed intervention.

A conference, at Bloemfontein in the Orange Free State, was led by President Kruger and the British High Commissioner of Cape Colony, Sir Alfred (later Lord) Milner; it was a failure. Compromises were offered and refused. Finally Kruger demanded that all troops be withdrawn from the Transvaal border, all newly-arrived reinforcements must leave South Africa, and that further reinforcements still at sea must not disembark.

The British government, irrevocably committed to helping the *uitlanders,* its whole existence in South Africa threatened, and unable to withstand a home public in the high noon of its Imperialism, rejected Kruger's 48-hour ultimatum.

At 5 p.m. on 11 October 1899, the South African War began.

General Buller sailed from England to command the British army. He left Waterloo station, in London, with an impressive farewell. The police held off crowds who threatened to mob him; they sang "Rule Britannia". Cabinet Ministers had come from Whitehall. His Royal Highness the Prince of Wales (later King Edward VII) had come from Buckingham Palace. A national hero, the beau ideal of a Victorian general, was on his way to settle a small local difficulty.

Three traumatic months were to pass before he signalled his intention to attack Spion Kop.

2 Prelude to the Battle: People, Places and Plans

The South African War was another which would be "over by Christmas". By then, however, there had been devastating defeats. More than 900 soldiers had surrendered at Nicholson's Nek, six miles north of Ladysmith. At Magersfontein (some 20 miles from Kimberley), at Stormberg (north of East London), and at Colenso (on the Tugela River), the élite of the army had been defeated by untrained farmers and burghers. Mafeking and Kimberley were besieged. Ladysmith was surrounded and was soon to be besieged as well.

These reverses muted hysterical British enthusiasm and destroyed the idolized picture of that national hero, General Sir Redvers Buller, VC.

When he had been appointed Commander-in-Chief South Africa, some people would have preferred another military hero and living legend, the great Field Marshal Lord Roberts of Kandahar. But he was not a favourite of the Commander-in-Chief of the whole British army, the powerful and influential Viscount Wolseley whose constant support of Buller had persuaded politicians and public that he was cast in the mould of Marlborough and Wellington.

Buller's military record was almost impeccable. He had served with Wolseley in the Canadian Red River Expedition, the Ashanti War, and the abortive Gordon Relief Expedition. He had won a much publicized Victoria Cross in the Zulu War, been Chief of Staff to General (later Field Marshal) Sir Evelyn Wood, VC, in the Boer War of 1881,

and head of the Intelligence Department in Egypt.

But he had never held supreme command on active service and he was reluctant to do so. When he was appointed to South Africa, in 1899, he told the Secretary of War that "I was better as a second in a complex military affair than as an officer in chief command", and added that for South Africa a better combination would be Viscount Wolseley in supreme command, with himself as Chief of Staff.

When he arrived at Cape Town, he was under heavy pressure from London to relieve Kimberley. The powerful and influential Cecil Rhodes, whose De Beers diamond mines were the main source of his vast wealth, had misled the government to believe that the fall of Kimberley was imminent. Buller sent Lieutenant General Lord Methuen to relieve it; General Gatacre, with a much-reduced force, was sent to occupy Stormberg and protect the route to East London; Lieutenant General Clery, with one Brigade, to meet the threat of rebellion in Natal. Buller led the Ladysmith relief force.

In one disastrous week Gatacre was defeated at Stormberg with a loss of 26 killed, 680 captured and wounded. Methuen was defeated at Magersfontein with a loss of some 200 killed, 730 wounded and missing. Buller was defeated at Colenso with a loss of 145 killed and more than 1,200 wounded and missing.

Strategically, Colenso was the most significant. Success would have relieved besieged and disease-ridden Ladysmith. When the action failed, Buller sent an astounding message to its defender, General Sir George White, VC, just a dozen miles away: "I tried Colenso yesterday but failed; the enemy too strong for my forces, except with siege operations, and those will take one month in preparation. Can you last so long? If not, how many days can you give me in which to take up defensive positions? After which I suggest your firing away as much ammunition as you can, and making best terms as you can."

If this astonished the gallant, hard-pressed Sir George White, who rejected the surrender suggestion, there was dismay in London when another signal arrived from Buller: "My view is that I ought to let Ladysmith go, and occupy good positions for defence of . . . Natal and let time help me . . . I now feel I cannot say I can relieve Ladysmith with my available force, and the best thing I can suggest is that I should occupy defensive positions and fight it out in a country better suited to our tactics."

After his defeat at Magersfontein, Lord Methuen had indicated that Kimberley could not be relieved before the end of February. Official reaction to those three defeats of "Black Week", and to the messages about Ladysmith, was swift. Buller was replaced as Commander-in-Chief; incredibly, he was not recalled but put in command of the Natal Field Force. The announcement was terse but tactful: "That as General Buller's hands were full in Natal the supervision and direction of the whole campaign should be placed in the hands of Lord Roberts with Lord Kitchener as Chief of Staff . . ."

Inexplicably, Lord Roberts left Buller to himself as Commander of the Natal Field Force. He certainly seemed to be well placed. With the newly arrived 5th Division, under Lieutenant General Sir Charles Warren, he had some 30,000 troops along the Tugela River.

No one could ever be certain about the Boer strength. British intelligence estimated that about 80,000 in all were mobilized, of whom perhaps 50,000 were under arms, with the addition of 2,000 European mercenaries. Between 10,000 and 12,000 Boers were believed to occupy the Tugela Heights and the land immediately to the north of it.

They had no uniforms. In the field, they wore slouch hats and their civilian clothes. Dressed for a formal group photograph, they looked like comic-opera bandits, with a variety of headgear that included much prized bowler hats. The bullet-filled, shoulder-slung bandolier was standard equipment.

Hard-riding, ill-disciplined individualists, they would fight and then ride off to their farms. They were not organized in regular companies, battalions or squadrons but in district commandos. They chose their own targets to create a British jibe that "every Boer was his own general".

For the most part, officers had little authority. Decisions were made democratically at a *Kriegsraad,* or Council of War. But as the campaign developed, outstanding natural leaders inevitably took responsibilities. Three of them consistently imposed their authority on the chaotic democracy of a People's Army: Christian de Wet, Piet Cronjé and, one of the most underestimated leaders in military history, Louis Dantje Botha.

In sharp contrast, Buller's troops were welded to an unquestioning disciplinary system. Although some of them were soldiers because of family links, the bulk of the rankers were refugees from poverty, squalor, and unemployment. Primitive and harsh as it was, the army offered a job (at a shilling a day for privates) and a home of sorts in an all-embracing Regiment.

They fought in remote lands for causes about which they knew little and generally cared nothing. Their patriotism was innate and unassailable. Out of the line they were heavy drinkers who fought among themselves. In the line they were men of matchless courage; a Boer admitted that "the British fight to kill, we fight to live."

The officers who commanded them were too often unworthy of their bravery and devotion. The regular officer who genuinely cared for their welfare was an exception.

One of those exceptions was General Buller.

To a man, his warrant-officers, non-commissioned officers, and private soldiers responded to his care of them with real affection, intense personal loyalty, and genuine self-sacrifice. Neither the Colenso defeat, nor the appointment of Lord Roberts, had diminished their faith in "old fighting Buller". He was a hero even to the newly-formed 5th Division. His living standards in the field were extravagantly high, with a keen enjoyment of fine food and champagne. A soldier's soldier, he always made sure of his troops' comfort and welfare.

Now, at his command post at Mount Alice, on Spearman's Hill, 17 miles west of Colenso, he knew that their steadfastness and loyalty were high among his assets. He believed that they and he had learnt to outwit and outshoot the Boers. The untried 5th Division would find confidence from their battle-hardened comrades. Despite Colenso, and his having been superseded by Lord Roberts, General Buller was uncharacteristically optimistic.

He did not underestimate the Boers. He knew their rifle shooting could be fatally accurate. Their Mausers might not be technically superior to the British Lee-Enfield and Lee-Metford but their deadly sharp-shooting and sniping had surprised an army whose musketry training had scarcely changed from the days of Inkerman. The un-coordinated mobility of the Boers' skilful fieldcraft made them elusively dangerous. Their stalking and killing of the springbok had been a perfect preparation for killing "Red Neck" soldiers.

Their rifle fire was supported by the quick-firing Vickers-Maxim machine guns, the

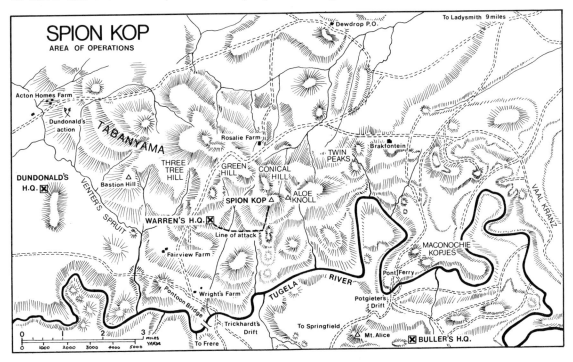

"pom-poms", with their 1 lb shells. Their artillery – the 94-pounder French Creusot siege guns (to become famous in ordnance history as the "Long Toms"), the 65 mm German Krupp and the Creusot quick-firing field guns – brought murderous fire on close-packed, static British troops. The use of smokeless powder, unconventional siting, masked target-spotting and counter-battery fire. Unlike the British, the Boers did not group their guns six in a line but sited them individually.

From his 1,000 ft high command post General Buller considered these factors as he faced the intimidating panorama of the Tugela Heights, 3-4 miles away across the river.

From left to right were the tactical features of Acton Homes Farm, some 10 miles to the west, the highlands of Tabanyama Ridge, Bastion Hill, Three Tree Hill, Green Hill, Conical Hill, Aloe Knoll, Twin Peaks, and Brakfontein Ridge. In front of Conical Hill, the 1,470 ft high Spion Kop dominated the panorama.

Two roads linked the Heights to Ladysmith: one, on the east side of Brakfontein Ridge; the other, on the west flank, to the left of Tabanyama through Acton Homes Farm. A third road, across Brakfontein itself, joined the others.

Buller, determined to avoid the tragic mistakes of Colenso, took several days to make his appreciation of the situation and a plan. Colenso had been lost because of a hurried and poor reconnaissance, inadequate orders, and an ill-conceived plan (of which *The Times History of the War in South Africa* said "a worst plan could not have been devised").

He put General Sir Charles Warren in command of the spearhead attack on the Heights.

The fast-flowing Tugela was sufficiently narrow everywhere for crossing by pontoons; at its narrowest part, by Trickhardt's Drift, it was only 80 yards wide and could be forded by troops swimming their horses.

A battle which makes an indelible mark on history may last a week, a day, or even a few hours. Its planning, the probing of enemy defences, diversionary attacks and sorties, and the advance to contact, are integral to it and generally decide its fate. Spion Kop was no exception.

On 17 January, 1,400 cavalry under Lieutenant General the Earl of Dundonald crossed the river. Behind them, General Warren put his infantry and artillery over the pontoons. By nightfall good tactical positions had been secured on virtually undefended ground below the Heights. On the following day, Warren's main force completed the crossing.

While he was trying to make a turning movement, two of his brigades were carrying out diversionary, frontal movements from Potgieter's Drift, 5 miles to the east. Intense Boer shelling failed to halt a steady advance. But the elaborate manoeuvring had been too slow. Nevertheless, by the evening of 20 January, despite the loss of some 100 men and a significant failure to turn the Boers' right flank, Warren had reached his first objectives.

Across 2,000 yards of steep, rocky, rivulet-patterned ground with its kopjes and boulders lay the final selected objective – the summit of Spion Kop.

On the morning of 22 January, General Buller sent his signal to London, "which," wrote Arthur Conan Doyle in *The Great Boer War,* "left the whole Empire in a hush of anticipation."

3 Secretly, by Night: Surprise at the Summit

High on the jagged Tugela Heights, the Boers had watched the tortuous British march from Frere, where General Buller had concentrated after Colenso. At first light on 10 January, with cavalry scouts ranging ahead, his immense column began its 23 mile advance to a rendezvous in the Springfield, Spearman's Hill, Potgieter's Drift, Trickhardt's Drift area on the south bank of the Tugela.

From their outposts overlooking the river the Boers were amazed to see this cumbersome force. Their own transport was confined to a few wagons. They had no formal lines of communication.

General Buller had 30,000 troops, eight field batteries, ten naval guns, and 650 vehicles drawn by horses, oxen, mules, and steam traction. The critical, precocious young war correspondent, Winston Spencer Churchill, reported: "The vast amount of baggage this army takes with it on the march hampers it movements."

Despite rain-flooded roads and overflowing *spruits* (rivers), Buller's force reached its rendezvous by 15 January. After some skirmishes with Boer picquets, the cavalry secured Mount Alice on Spearman's Hill. On 17 and 18 January General Warren's troops crossed the river. Except for one decisive move he then wasted invaluable hours manoeuvring the main body instead of making a swift attack on Tabanyama Ridge. On 18 January the watching Boers were joined by their commander, Louis Botha.

Born a British subject in Natal, son of an original *voortrekker,* the 37-year-old farmer and lawyer had no military training; but he had first seen active service in 1887. A natural leader, he was better educated, more intelligent, and more prosperous than the men he led. In contrast to the other burghers and farmers, he was dapper and smartly dressed. He had the vanity and self-confidence of every successful commander. A total defeat of Buller at Colenso had proved that his personal leadership could turn an undisciplined rabble into a victorious fighting unit. He was confident that he could defeat this new threat to relieve Ladysmith.

But it was a cautious confidence. He knew that the odds were against him and that he was out-numbered by famous battle-experienced regiments. He had fewer weapons. He knew that he would have to inspire and rally his men again. He feared and respected the courage and indominatable spirit of the British regimental soldier. Later, he was to write of the Irish Brigade at Colenso: " . . . No less than five times they charged, and I never want to see finer bravery than I saw then."

In some hard fighting below the Heights, after General Warren had crossed the river, he had seen that courage and resolution again. By itself it had not been enough. Poor deployment and indecision had blunted the British attacks. Although supported by intense artillery fire, the soldiers had never breached his forward defensive trench system.

The Boers had faltered under the heavy but mostly inaccurate gun fire, but Botha rallied them, steadied them, and kept them in position. He was determined to keep his force intact in the Tabanyama area, which was the core of his defence. He would not be drawn out of it to fight a main battle or to counter attack. He skilfully pulled his outposts back. His tactics were simple: to hold his main effort in his mountain fortress until he could trap the British into too small a space, where they could be contained. Every Boer could then choose his own killing ground.

With his quick, inborn military instinct, he knew that the British had lost the first round. But he knew, too, that they might easily have won it.

A cavalry reconnaissance at his exposed, lightly-held right flank, at Acton Homes Farm, had surprised and ambushed some 300 Boers, 50 of whom had been killed or captured. Rapid consolidation and reinforcement of this success with infantry, artillery, and additional cavalry would have turned the flank and captured the road to Ladysmith which ran behind the Boers' positions. To Botha's surprise the only reinforcements had been a small cavalry force.

If this minor action had been exploited, Ladysmith could have been relieved and there would have been no great battle of history. The failure, General Warren's ponderous manoeuvrings below the Heights, and his abortive attack on Tabanyama, sharply exposed the latent hostility between General Buller and his second in command.

From his command post at Mount Alice, the phlegmatic Buller had been shaken out of his characteristic lethargy. He believed that his orders had been clear and decisive. Warren believed that they allowed him considerable discretion.

General Buller had decided that the Boer positions opposite Potgieter's Drift were too strong to be captured by direct attack. "I intend," he said in his orders to General Warren, "to try to turn it by sending a force across the Tugela from near Trickhardt's Drift, and up to the west of Spion Kop . . . You

will, of course, act as circumstances require, but my idea is that you should continue throughout, refusing your right and throwing your left forward until you gain the open plain north of Spion Kop. Once there you will command the position facing Potgieter's Drift, and I think render it untenable . . . I shall endeavour to keep up heliograph communication with you from a post on the hill directly in your rear."

Three of the basic principles of an operation order are Intention, Method, and Intercommunication. The Intention, to attack up the west of Spion Kop, was clear. The Method was obscure. The lack of Intercommunication was to be a vital and decisive part of the forthcoming battle.

The uncertainty, ambiguity, and imprecision of Buller's orders, the lack of authority in the wording, had unquestionably given General Warren a wide discretion. The secrets of the remote Spion Kop area could be revealed only by maps and reconnaissance. But no maps were available, and no detailed reconnaissance was made. But there were at least four ways of going "up to the west of Spion Kop": the west face itself; a ravine between the Kop and Tabanyama; the road over the eastern end of Tabanyama, through Fairview Farm and across the high ground northeast to Rosalie Farm; westwards, on the Boers' exposed flank at Acton Homes Farm.

Liaison between the two commanders was a pre-ordained failure. General Warren was an unwelcome addition to Buller's staff. He had been sent to South Africa not only as commander of the 5th Division but also as a possible replacement for Buller, who regarded Warren's appointment with brooding suspicion. Moreover, General Warren was a Sapper. Although he had been trained at the Royal Military College, Sandhurst, and the Royal Military Academy, Woolwich, he had no field experience of commanding infantry, cavalry, and artillery. A distinguished army surveyor, he had seen active service against the Boers in the Transkei, served with the British army in Egypt, been Chief Commissioner of London's Metropolitan Police, and then in command at Straits Settlements. He had tried unsuccessfully to become a Member of Parliament. The apex of his career to date was the knighthood he received from Queen Victoria for distinguished service in the Sinai Desert, which included the arrest of the murderer of a British priest.

With this patchwork of a reputation he had been appointed to command the 5th Division – to everyone's surprise including his own. He had retired from the army when the South African War had begun, but Viscount Wolseley recalled him, gave him the 5th Division, made him Buller's second in command, and dispatched him to the Cape. When he arrived, fresh orders instructed him to take over from Lord Methuen as commander of the Kimberley Relief Force. Just 24 hours later these orders were also cancelled and he was instructed to join General Buller. Whitehall had agreed to an urgent signal request from Buller to retain Methuen; in exchange Buller received the 5th Division as a welcome reinforcement and its commander as an unwanted comrade.

Warren's time-wasting manoeuvres once he had crossed the Tugela emphasized his inexperience and lack of confidence. "It seemed", wrote an officer in the Somerset Light Infantry, "as if we were carrying out summer manoeuvres in the Long Valley at Aldershot."

The failure to turn the Boer flank at Acton Homes Farm was the result of Warren's ineptitude and inability to handle cavalry. A gallant and dashing officer, Lieutenant General the Earl of Dundonald had ambushed the Boer patrol at Acton Homes Farm. He soon realized that if he could hold the Acton Homes Farm road he could also secure the road to Ladysmith. With this, and the Boer flank turned, Major General Lyttleton's Brigade and parts of Warren's main force could mount a major attack and open the way

British Sappers building a pontoon bridge in South Africa (*National Army Museum*).

to Ladysmith.

But Warren's only response was to send one and a half squadrons of the Royals (1st The Royal Dragoons), to be followed later with an order for Dundonald to withdraw and protect his headquarters. Dundonald's success was brief, and a decisive opportunity had been thrown away.

The hostility between Buller and his second in command reached a crisis. General Buller changed his mind about relieving Warren of his command. Instead, on 22 January he gave him the choice of attacking Spion Kop without further delay.

To this day, there is confusion about who decided on that historic and momentous objective. We know that General Warren wanted to break through the Heights via the Fairview-Rosalie Farm road; that he told General Buller it was impossible to do so without first securing Spion Kop. Buller's curious, casual reply, "Of course you must take it," can perhaps be misjudged out of its contemporary context. But as Commander-in-Chief he alone was responsible for the decision.

These were virtually the last days in British military history when generals personally led their troops into battle. General Warren has been severely criticized for not having done so. In fact, his offer was rejected by General Buller who could not rely on a man he had almost dismissed. In any event, it would have been wrong if Buller had agreed, unless he himself was willing to move forward from his command post across the river. General Warren's responsibility was to direct and control. His offer to lead, though well meant, was misplaced and revealed, again, his lack of leadership.

The immediate Spion Kop attack which General Buller had ordered was delayed. The game-legged Major General Coke had been selected by Warren to command the main effort, with Major General Woodgate's Lancashire Brigade leading. Quite rightly, Coke asked for a day's postponement so that he could reconnoitre the ground and rest his troops. General Warren agreed . . . but omitted to tell General Buller. On his way back to his camp from Warren's Task Force headquarters, the unhappy Coke lost his way in the darkness and spent the night on the open veldt.

At sunrise, General Buller, who had spent the night in a comfortable, untroubled sleep, was angrily astonished at the postponement. He put General Woodgate in command of the spearhead.

His brigade was composed of the 2nd Battalion The King's Own Royal Lancaster Regiment, the 2nd Battalion The Lancashire Fusiliers, 1st Battalion The Prince of Wales's Volunteers (South Lancashire), 1st Battalion The York and Lancaster Regiment, supported by the 7th, 78th, and 73rd batteries Royal Field Artillery, one squadron 13th Hussars, the Mounted Infantry (dismounted), and a half company of 37th Company Royal Engineers.

In rain and thickening mist, under a dark starless night sky, Woodgate's Brigade assembled in the Wright's Farm-Trickhardt's Drift area. Orders for the approach were strict and explicit: no talking, no lights, no shooting – any outlying Boer picquets were to be dealt with by bayonets only.

Although the sound of nailed boots on the rocky ground could not be concealed from the enemy, it would not reveal the line of march; the Boers knew that a large force was concentrated below them and that an attack was almost imminent. They thought, however, that it would probably come at dawn; the sound of clambering boots and rattling equipment would not be unusual.

Two experienced officers were the pathfinders; Lieutenant Colonel Thorneycroft commanding the Mounted Infantry, and Lieutenant Colonel Bloomfield commanding 2nd Lancashire Fusiliers.

The long, hard, sweating climb in single file began at 10.30 p.m., but to cover any outlying Boer picquets extended order was adopted as the column approached the objective.

But there were no picquets, not even a single Boer sentry post until Spion Kop was reached at 3.30 a.m. Suddenly, out of the misty darkness, there was a warning shout in Dutch followed by a burst of Mauser fire. The Mounted Infantry and the Lancashire Fusiliers charged with fixed bayonets. The Boer defenders from the Vryheid commando scrambled away into the darkness.

No need now for silence and secrecy. The soldiers' cheers – a previously-arranged victory signal – echoed over the veldt to Warren's Task Force headquarters and across the river to General Buller's command post.

It was 4.30 a.m. Spion Kop was seemingly captured. The brief skirmish had lasted only three minutes. Three British soldiers had been wounded.

4 The Battle: First Phase

On the reverse slope of Tabanyama Ridge a lightly-sleeping Louis Botha, shocked into wide-awake alertness by the shooting on the crest, persuaded, cajoled, and bullied the fleeing burghers to stay and fight. Even those who were already harnessing their horses to the laagered wagons were put into the line. He was supported by the energetic and equally-aggressive Commandant Henrik Prinsloo.

Botha could not tell if this was a diversionary attack to draw off a main thrust. Thick mist, holding back the dawn and early sunrise, obscured the British intentions and dispositons.

Swift, decisive action was essential to repulse or hold the consolidation that must surely exploit the British success. He sent the Pretoria and Carolina commandos under Commandants Opperman and Prinsloo to reinforce the summit. More reinforcements were summoned from outlying areas. He called up the 94-pounder Creusot fortress guns, the 65 mm Krupp and Creusot quick-firing field guns. The Vickers-Maxim pompoms, with their 1 lb shells, supplemented the Mausers. He covered his vulnerable left flank.

By 7.00 a.m., with the heavy mist slowly clearing, a deadly arc of fire from Green Hill, Conical Hill, Aloe Knoll, and Twin Peaks, threatened the British consolidation and exploitation.

But there was no consolidation or exploitation. No fighting or reconnaissance patrols or scouts crept forward under cover of the mist.

Although Botha was unaware of it, General Woodgate had halted the advance at the moment of apparent victory. Having, as he believed, captured his objective, he intended to repulse any Boer counter-attack from a defensive position. The Royal Engineers hacked desperately to dig shallow trenches on the hard, unresponsive, rocky ground. By 4.00 a.m., as dawn could be glimpsed through the mist, the trenches were uncompleted. The mist however formed a brief, welcome screen against the rising sun.

When the mist did clear, at 7.30 a.m., it revealed an awesome situation.

Spion Kop had not been captured. Instead, the highest part of the plateau had been mistaken for the crest. The British were trapped and crowded into a position that would have been a serious threat to 500 troops; but some 1,700 soldiers were there, mercilessly exposed, holding only half the plateau, with a field of fire that rarely exceeded 100 yards.

Several attacks were made to drive the Boers back, and some limited gains were made. General Woodgate sent a reassuring message to General Warren at Task Force headquarters, on Three Tree Hill, 3 miles away. It also contained a request for the Royal Artillery 15-pounder guns to be hauled up and for Lyttleton's Brigade to attack Twin Peaks.

It is inconceivable that Woodgate could have sent so complacent a message. His modest counter-attacks had achieved only a limited success. The clearing mist still obscured the entire area, in particular Aloe

Knoll. The Boers still held the British in fatal fire trap.

By the time Woodgate's situation report had reached General Warren, complacency turned to tragedy . . .

Botha was dumbfounded by the British tactics and positions. This untrained, natural soldier could scarcely believe that these Sandhurst-trained leaders could have made such a blunder. Even if the objective had been mistaken, a rapid consolidation and exploitation before daylight could have turned error into victory.

Botha had planned to draw the British into this fire trap; incredibly, they had walked into it. An even greater surprise awaited him. The bright morning sunshine etched the battlefield and the British dispositions in sharp detail . . . and he realized that Spion Kop was being attacked in isolation. It was a concentration of effort in the wrong place.

Napoleon is said to have asked for "lucky generals", by which he meant those who had the skill, resolution, and initiative to capitalize on enemy mistakes. By that definition, Louis Botha was a very lucky general indeed.

Botha organized incessant attacks not only to stem the British forays from their trenches but also to contain them there. As the three Krupp guns thundered from Green Hill, supported by the pom-poms, the Carolina commando rushed the British forward positions. After some savage, close-quarter fighting, with the Lancashire men using the bodies of their dead comrades as ramparts, the forward elements were driven back. The Carolina commando, joined now by those of the Heidelberg, had space to use their natural fieldcraft. Using a copy-book manoeuvre of fire and movement, they brought Mauser fire to bear from three different areas.

The British soldiers were traditionally trained to fire on command volleys. Now however in the chaos of close-quarter, hand-to-hand fighting, their lack of training in individual marksmanship was a fatal handicap against an enemy who shot at selected, individual targets.

The Kop was swept by devastating small arms and artillery fire. As the Mauser bullets, pom-pom shells, and artillery shells and shrapnel brought heavy casualties, the Royal Artillery in the valley below opened a counter-bombardment.

And not the least of the tragedies of that fateful morning, the range was short. Botha's own reference described the consequences. Writing later of "the astounding inefficiency" of the British artillery in contrast to his own, he said: " . . . Our Krupps and pom-poms told with terrible effect on the massed Tommies on the narrow ledge. The English guns . . . were responsible for a large number of casualties on their own side . . ."

Subsequent attempts have been made to vindicate the artillery's reputation at Spion Kop. Down at Gun Hill, with a field of fire that could cover the whole Boer front, there were six batteries: the 7th, 19th, 63rd, 73rd, and 78th of the Royal Field Artillery, and the 61st Howitzer Battery. Their main target, the enemy artillery, was certainly masked by a hill; but adequate maps, observation posts, and reconnaissance before the battle would have led to better siting.

The 4.7-inch naval guns at Mount Alice were also out of effective range.

More serious even than the short-range shelling was the absence of a Mountain Battery. Nothing exemplifies the lack of planning and staff work than the incident of the missing battery. Whatever final objective was to be selected, everyone knew that the Heights must be taken. Everyone should have known that a Mountain Battery was indispensable. But it remained at Frere.

General Woodgate's complacency and miscalculation were soon changed. Desperately pressed, he sent a message to General Buller on Mount Alice: "Am exposed to terrible cross fire . . . can barely hold our own. Water badly needed. Help us."

Deneys Reitz was one of Louis Botha´s most reliable and efficient subordinates. A Pretoria commando, he was a leader not only in the savage hand-to-hand fighting at Spion Kop but also in successfully rallying the retreating Boers when all seemed lost. He was the author of one of the few books about the South African War written from the Boer viewpoint. It is notable for its accuracy and fairness to both sides.

Lieutenant General Sir Charles Warren led the 5th Division at Spion Kop and was therefore the immediate battlefield commander as well. A Sapper, with a distinguished army reputation for surveying and staff work, he went to Spion Kop with no field experience in commanding infantry, cavalry, and artillery. A man of varied interests and ambitions, he had previously served in South Africa, Egypt, the Straits Settlements; been Chief Commissioner of London's Metropolitan Police; and tried unsuccessfully to become a Member of Parliament. His uneasy relationship with his Commander-in-Chief, General Sir Redvers Buller, culminated in his being relieved of his command after Spion Kop and sent back to England.

A dismounted Boer commando. Equally effective in the saddle or stalking in the veldt, the commandos were pioneers in fieldcraft, expert scouts who knew every yard of their territory, and accurate marksmen. Forced into remote areas by *uitlander* penetration, their ancestors had learnt to kill a running buck from the saddle at 400 yards. Dismounted, they had learnt to stalk their prey at close quarters. Their descendants used these skills with deadly effect against the British in South Africa.

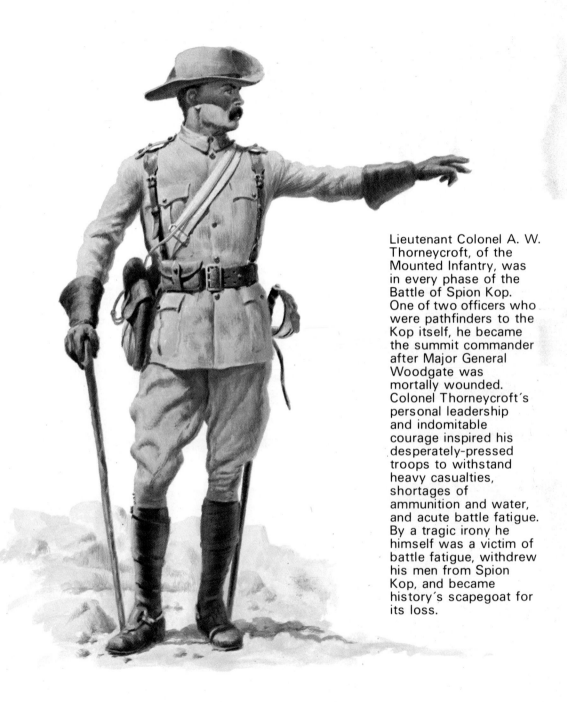

Lieutenant Colonel A. W. Thorneycroft, of the Mounted Infantry, was in every phase of the Battle of Spion Kop. One of two officers who were pathfinders to the Kop itself, he became the summit commander after Major General Woodgate was mortally wounded. Colonel Thorneycroft's personal leadership and indomitable courage inspired his desperately-pressed troops to withstand heavy casualties, shortages of ammunition and water, and acute battle fatigue. By a tragic irony he himself was a victim of battle fatigue, withdrew his men from Spion Kop, and became history's scapegoat for its loss.

Louis Botha, commander of the Boers at Spion Kop, earned immortal fame there as a great general. A farmer and lawyer, with no military training, he had an instinct for leadership and tactics. He snatched victory from almost certain defeat, outwitted and outfought British generals who had long campaigning experience. He survived the South African War to be invited by King Edward VII to become the first Prime Minister of the Union of South Africa. He led the Union into World War I as Britain's ally.

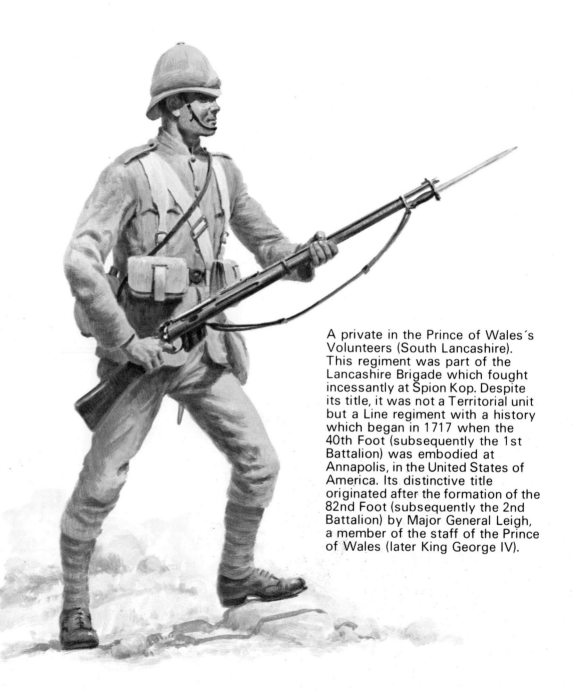

A private in the Prince of Wales's Volunteers (South Lancashire). This regiment was part of the Lancashire Brigade which fought incessantly at Spion Kop. Despite its title, it was not a Territorial unit but a Line regiment with a history which began in 1717 when the 40th Foot (subsequently the 1st Battalion) was embodied at Annapolis, in the United States of America. Its distinctive title originated after the formation of the 82nd Foot (subsequently the 2nd Battalion) by Major General Leigh, a member of the staff of the Prince of Wales (later King George IV).

A mounted Boer commando. Although the word "commando" was wrongly used to describe all Boer soldiers, a commando was a unit formed from a particular district. None of the units was organized in regular companies, battalions, or squadrons. The Boer commandos were individualists who were difficult to control, resented formal discipline or orders, and earned a British jibe that "every Boer was his own general".

A trooper in the 13th Royal Hussars. This regiment was part of General Buller's unused reserves and took no part in the Spion Kop fighting. However, it earned a distinguished record elsewhere in the South African War of 1899-1902 and was engaged in the subsequent relief of Ladysmith. The regiment was raised in 1715, as the "Green Dragoons". It saw service in the West Indies under Abercromby in 1796, took part in the Maroon War in Jamaica in 1798, and was one of the five regiments which charged with the Light Brigade at Balaclava in the Crimean War. After World War I, the 13th and the 18th Hussars were amalgamated to form the 13th-18th Royal Hussars (Queen Mary's Own).

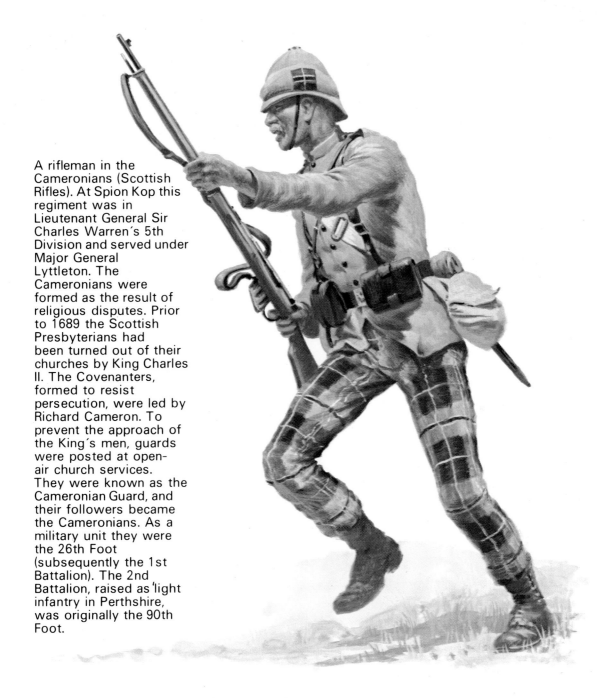

A rifleman in the Cameronians (Scottish Rifles). At Spion Kop this regiment was in Lieutenant General Sir Charles Warren's 5th Division and served under Major General Lyttleton. The Cameronians were formed as the result of religious disputes. Prior to 1689 the Scottish Presbyterians had been turned out of their churches by King Charles II. The Covenanters, formed to resist persecution, were led by Richard Cameron. To prevent the approach of the King's men, guards were posted at open-air church services. They were known as the Cameronian Guard, and their followers became the Cameronians. As a military unit they were the 26th Foot (subsequently the 1st Battalion). The 2nd Battalion, raised as 'light infantry in Perthshire, was originally the 90th Foot.

A Royal Artillery field gunner shown here with leather-covered steel reinforcement to the outside of the legging to protect his leg from the harness and shaft of his team horse. The whitewood-handle whip was a long, plaited lash used to control the team horse by being "laid on" its withers without hitting it. Six batteries of the Royal Field Artillery were in action at Spion Kop, but the gunners' gallantry and steadfastness did not match their shooting and siting which were later severely criticized. Field Marshal Lord Roberts complained that the guns were inferior in range, firing, and accuracy to the Boer Creusot and Krupp ordnance.

A Staats-Artillerie
(Transvaal State
Artillery) gunner. Part of
the Boer regular forces,
the State Artillery
surprised the British in
the South African War by
the quality and
accuracy of their
shooting. In contrast to
the British six-gun-
grouping, the State
Artillery were more
mobile and flexible in
their gun handling. This,
together with the use of
smokeless powder,
reduced the
effectiveness of the
Royal Artillery´s
observation and
counter-battery fire.
Among the most
formidable of the guns
used by the State
Artillery at Spion Kop
were the 94-pounder
French Creusot (the
"Long Tom") and the
64 mm German Krupp.

This 37 mm German-made Krupp was part of
the Boer artillery in the South African
War. It fired 1 lb shells at 300 rounds a
minute and had an effective range of 3,000
yards. Having no manufacturing
resources the Boers obtained their best
weapons from Germany and France. The
German officer, Major Albrecht, in charge
of the Free State Artillery for nearly 20
years was mainly responsible for its accurate
shooting, tactical gun handling, and
selection of weapons. The formality and
smartness of the Artillery men's uniforms
shown here is in sharp contrast to the
informal dress of the commandos
illustrated on pages 19 and 23.

An observation post with heliograph and telescope. A major communications device in the South African War, the heliograph was an instrument used for signalling swiftly between two distant points by flashing the sun's rays from the face of a mirror. The flashes followed each other in a pre-arranged signal code. The mirror, with part of the mercury back removed, was mounted on a tripod, and two sights were provided in front with a screen. The sun ray was then directed through both sights and the flash could be seen many miles away; the range of the flash depended on the size of the mirror, but distances of 40-50 miles were not uncommon.

A Royal Artillery Mountain Battery, with its 2.7 Howitzer. This
gun could be broken down into separate loads and
carried by mules and horses. In high, rocky or mountainous
country, through precipitous passes and defiles, the
Mountain battery's guns were the infantry's only close-
support artillery. A blunder prevented the Mountain battery
reaching the hard-pressed soldiers at Spion Kop, where their
long-range artillery was a failure.

General Buller´s force
which advanced to the
rendezvous for the
Battle of Spion Kop
included 650 vehicles
drawn by oxen – as
illustrated above –
horses, mules and
steam tractors. The
administrative support
for some 30,000 troops
was cumbersome and
slow-moving. Winston
Churchill, who was a
war correspondent at
Spion Kop, wrote: "The
vast amount of
baggage this army
takes with it on the march
hampers its
movements."

This message highlights the poorly-coordinated command structure. General Warren was Woodgate's chief, and Warren himself was responsible to General Buller.

But the hapless Woodgate was never to receive a reply, from Buller or Warren. At 8.30 a.m. he was mortally wounded. As we shall see, the results of this have no parallel in military history.

As the next senior officer in the battle area, Lieutenant Colonel Bloomfield of the Lancashire Fusiliers took command. He was wounded almost immediately and replaced by Lieutenant Colonel Crofton of the King's Own Royal Lancaster Regiment. At about 10.00 a.m. he sent a message to General Warren which was also received by General Buller: "Reinforce at once or all lost. General dead." (In fact General Woodgate was to die later.)

Reinforcements were certainly not required in that overcrowded shambles of a fire trap. But General Warren sent them, from 2nd Battalion The Middlesex Regiment, 2nd Battalion The Dorsetshire Regiment, and the Imperial Light Infantry from Coke's Brigade.

Meanwhile, many gallant attempts were made to break out of the trap. The 6½ ft tall, 20-stone figure of Lieutenant Colonel Thorneycroft showed unbreakable courage and superb leadership. Although he was handicapped by a severely sprained ankle, he was always in the heat of the battle. He organized counter-attacks and kept the line in some sort of order.

Individual positions, only a few yards in extent, changed hands in bitter and savage close-quarter fighting. But the successes were few, and the Boers were never dislodged from their dominating ground.

Every battle has its soldiers whose endurance breaks, and at Spion Kop some gave in, although proved desertion could be punishable by death.

About 200 men of the Lancashire Fusiliers went forward to surrender to the Boers. Moral judgments on surrender or apparent cowardice are inappropriate except by people in the action. It is enough to say that the Fusiliers had been exposed to the full fury of the enfilade fire from the beginning, had withstood incessant Mauser, pom-pom, artillery attacks, and hand-to-hand fighting literally to the death. They were hemmed-in by corpses and their tenacity was sapped by the moans and cries of their dying and wounded comrades. They were without water in a noon temperature of 100° Fahrenheit.

Few things in warfare are more contagious than desertion, surrender, or individual retreat in the face of almost certain defeat. Colonel Thorneycroft saw this danger immediately. To him, soldiers were there to fight and not to surrender. He limped forward on his sprained ankle. The Boers, already taking away some of the Fusiliers, were awe-stricken by this bellowing giant of a soldier. "You may go to hell!" he is reported to have shouted. "I am in command here and allow no surrender!"

He rallied the remaining Fusiliers and ordered them to "go on shooting". He restored the line, with the help of his own Mounted Infantry and men from the Middlesex Regiment who had been separated from their comrades. He had stopped the contagion from spreading.

Like a spectator in a remote grandstand, General Buller had seen Thorneycroft's outstanding leadership. And he had been worried by Crofton's panic-like message. He heliographed Warren to make yet another command change: "Unless you put some really hard fighting man in command on the top, you will lose the hill. I suggest Thorneycroft."

And General Warren, having already put Coke in charge, heliographed the battle area: "With the approval of the Commander-in-Chief, I place Lieutenant Colonel Thorneycroft in command of the summit with the local rank of Brigadier General."

But he failed to tell Major General Coke that he had been superseded.

Coke himself was not the only officer who was unaware that there was a new commander. Some people alas never did realize it. Others, like Lieutenant Colonel Cooke, 2nd Battalion The Cameronians (Scottish Rifles), protested and demanded his gazette seniority, which was above that of Thorneycroft. We can only imagine how the rumbustious Acting Brigadier General silenced this jealous if natural protest. There were other officers, deeply respectful of hierarchy and Army List seniority, who knew that Lieutenant Colonel Hill of the 2nd Middlesex was senior to Crofton, Cooke, and Thorneycroft. Their support for him was endorsed by his having been made an Acting Brigadier General as well.

There was total confusion about the leadership. Throughout the battle some thought that Thorneycroft was in charge; some believed it was Cooke; some thought Crofton; others that it was Hill; and some thought it was the elusive Major General Coke.

Another senior officer, Major General the Honourable N. Lyttleton, waited impatiently in the wings. He had been expecting Warren to send his Brigade into action. His troops – 2nd Battalion The Cameronians (Scottish Rifles), 3rd Battalion The King's Royal Rifle Corps (60th Rifles), 1st Battalion The Durham Light Infantry, and 1st Battalion The Rifle Brigade – had already seen hard fighting after the crossing of the Tugela. They were now in reserve while Lyttleton watched the battle with dismay and anxiety. He could not know that there were too many soldiers there. From his viewpoint, and lacking any information, the plateau commander was desperately pressed.

His opinion was confirmed when, first, Warren asked him to reinforce the Kop and, then, when he picked up a heliograph appeal for help from the Kop itself.

He sent the Cameronians, together with the South African regiment, Bethune's Mounted Infantry. They were to be tested to their limits . . . but not with Brigadier General Thorneycroft.

There was no orderly, prepared plan to reinforce the Kop; no pre-arranged, co-ordinated assembly area or rendezvous; no clear line of approach. Lyttleton's reinforcements were diverted to another battle, together with the Middlesex Regiment and the Imperial Light Infantry. No one knew that this was quite separate from Thorneycroft's battle.

Thorneycroft himself, only perhaps 300-400 yards away, knew nothing of this second, subsidiary action. It came about almost by chance.

Some accounts of Spion Kop are misunderstood because the separation, the two distinct actions, are not emphasized or clearly explained. The main battle was fought on the upper plateau in the Lancashire Brigade area. The second was fought on the lower plateau, on the south-east face of the Kop. There was no co-ordination, no formal line or front.

Up on the true crest, Louis Botha, unlike his two British counterparts, directed the defence from the heart of the battle. His many preoccupations and lonely responsibility did not distract his analytical, calculating brain.

His tactical positions were still dominatingly secure; but his confidence that he could hold the British on the upper plateau was overshadowed by two anxieties. First, the British intentions and, second, the morale of his men.

Like every successful general, he tried to forecast the enemy's intentions. What would he do now if he were commanding the British force? He knew that they should extend their front considerably to attack his flanks at Twin Peaks and, farther away, at Acton Homes Farm, in a wide pincer movement.

He was anxiously puzzled why they had not done so, that they continued to fight Spion Kop in isolation. He knew that they had thousands of disengaged troops.

Again, the contrast between the two Sandhurst-Woolwich trained British leaders and the civilian with his innate military instinct is inescapable.

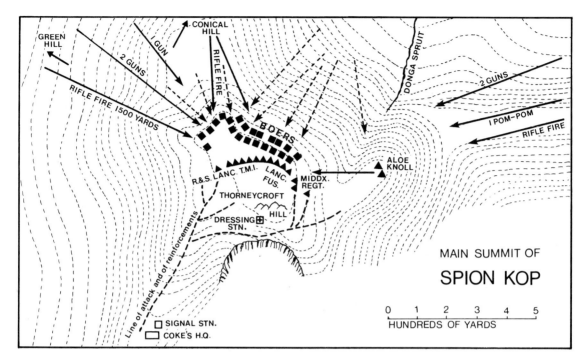

GREEN HILL

CONICAL HILL

2 GUNS

GUN

RIFLE FIRE

RIFLE FIRE 1500 YARDS

BOERS

DONGA SPRUIT

2 GUNS

1 POM-POM

RIFLE FIRE

ALOE KNOLL

R.&S. LANC. T.M.I. LANC. FUS. MIDDX. REGT.

THORNEYCROFT HILL

DRESSING STN.

Line of attack and of reinforcements

MAIN SUMMIT OF

SPION KOP

```
0   1   2   3   4   5
HUNDREDS OF YARDS
```

☐ SIGNAL STN.

▭ COKE'S H.Q.

If they did extend their front and attack in strength Botha knew that he could not hold them. Surely their lack of tactical sense could not continue? He was equally mystified by the remoteness and immobility of Warren and Buller. He knew that in fighting of this kind the physical presence of the commander was vital.

Inextricably linked with his anxiety about the British intentions was his worry about morale. Although his casualties were relatively small, he knew that he must defeat the brave, stubborn British troops on the plateau. His Boers' morale lived on quick success and withered under failure or prolonged fighting with no result.

To achieve that defeat he decided to attack the British left flank around Aloe Knoll. It was this which made the lower plateau the scene of the second action.

The subsequent battle for the flank, on the lower plateau, was no less bloody than that in Thorneycroft's sector; it was even more personal and one of brutal attrition. Individual Boer and Briton fought each other for the brief possession of a yard or so of ground, of a rock or sangar to give meagre cover. The mêlée and no quarter hand-to-hand fighting replaced controlled combat. With hindsight some historians have dismissed this as wasteful slaughter. But if Botha's attack had succeeded, Thorneycroft's flank would have been turned and the whole Kop would have been lost.

Not one British officer or other rank engaged in that grim struggle knew of its crucial importance to Thorneycroft. To them it was an extension of the rest of the fighting.

Even if Colonel (Acting Brigadier General) Hill, or anyone else on that lower plateau, had realized its importance and link, the overwhelming close-quarter fighting would have prevented any communication.

The flank attack failed. The Boers were held. Moreover one of Botha's anxieties had partly turned to reality. His weak flank, Twin Peak, had been captured during the afternoon. Now it was the Boers who were in danger of being turned and destroyed. The battle for the Kop itself had reached its climax. Victory was there to be grasped.

In his book *Commando* Deneys Reitz of the Pretoria commando wrote: "We were hungry, thirsty, and tired, and around us were the dead men covered with swarms of flies attracted by the smell of blood."

Morale was at its lowest. It is a decisive principle of warfare. Viscount Montgomery has described it as "the greatest single factor in war"; and in his orders before Alamein he wrote: "The final issue may well depend on which side can best last out and stand up to the buffetings, the ups and downs, and the continual strain of hard fighting . . ."

At Spion Kop, 42 years earlier, the British soldier won this particular battle of morale.

This artist's impression of the preliminary stages of the Battle of Spion Kop gives a realistic example of the harsh, rugged country (*Illustrated London News*).

5 The Battle: Final Phase

Throughout the day General Buller, immobile and detached at Mount Alice, had certainly been a delegating Commander-in-Chief. Apart from some ineffectual signalled advice, he left General Warren in dangerous isolation. And Warren himself, separated from the plateau fighting, failed to co-ordinate or control it. Except for one visit to the base of the Kop, he never went forward to direct the operations. He relied on heliograph, liaison officers, and runners for communications. Messages were garbled and misunderstood. Even when they were accurate, events had changed them when they arrived at Three Tree Hill.

Although he was seemingly ignorant of the confusion over the plateau command he never established an exclusive, direct communication with Brigadier General Thorneycroft. Warren had obeyed Buller's orders to appoint Thorneycroft as plateau commander, but he relied on his own choice of Major General Coke, whose reports proved to be disastrously inaccurate and misleading.

General Coke had taken a very long time to reach the battle area after General Warren had sent him there as overall commander, before Thorneycroft's appointment. Even then, he never went to Thorneycroft's position where he would have learnt the unwelcome news that he had been superseded. Instead he remained closer to the flank action when that developed, and spent most of his time in his own command post on a sheltered ledge, some distance from any of the fighting. He was therefore effectively out of touch with everyone and every phase of the battle. Long after Spion Kop was over, there were allegations against him of cowardice.

He did, however, see a message from Thorneycroft to General Warren. It was ominous, if anyone had taken it seriously. It asked for reinforcements. The Lancashire Brigade and the Mounted Infantry, Thorneycroft said, were "quite done up", not only because of the fighting but also because of the scorching temperatures and shortage of water. Ammunition was short too. He said that reinforcements were useless unless the Boers could be contained. His message ended: "If you wish to hold the hill for the night you must send more infantry and attack enemy's guns."

But General Coke had already decided that no more reinforcements were required. He did not know that Thorneycroft's troops were exhausted or of the extent of their casualties, or that Thorneycroft needed fresh replacements rather then reinforcements. Because he did know that better artillery support was not immediately possible, General Coke did not endorse the request for it.

Satisfied that the flank attack on the lower plateau was being held, mistaking it for the main action, he sent Thorneycroft's appeal to the supine Warren with a misleading message that the day was going well.

The British artillery continued to be ineffective. We have seen already that its siting and ranging were fatally inaccurate. Improvement could be made only if the batteries were brought forward to higher ground.

The Gunners said it was impossible to do this unless a route was prepared through the rocky, boulder-strewn ground. The infantry commanders, and they were supported by Winston Churchill, believed that it could be done with resolution and determination.

The Gunners were right. But no excuses can be made for the bad pre-battle planning and reconnaissance. Buller may have been justified in leaving dispositions to Warren. And Warren may have been justified in leaving artillery dispositions to the Commander Royal Artillery. It is undeniable, however, that someone should have carried out correct range-finding, reconnaissance, and siting during the wasted days of manoeuvre . . . the dress rehearsal for Spion Kop. The Royal Engineers could then have prepared a track to the battle area.

Thorneycroft's request did not receive a reply from Warren. Instead, while he was attempting a gallantly-despairing counter-attack on the crest, Coke sent an order to "the officer commanding the upper plateau" to stop any further advance.

Much later, when the battle was over, he realized that he had sent an order to his own commanding officer.

Help was to come to Thorneycroft from another quarter.

Down at Potgieter's Drift, Major General Lyttleton had continued to watch the battle with a true professional soldier's judgment. He realized that the key to success was the capture of Twin Peaks, a mile to the east of Spion Kop. Except for Acton Homes Farm, which was beyond the battle area, the Peaks were the Boers' weakest-held defensive position.

Without consulting General Warren, General Buller, or even Thorneycroft, he sent 3rd Battalion The King's Royal Rifle Corps to attack the Peaks.

As this assault, and its consequences, became one of the most bitterly argued controversies, we must consider Lyttleton's motives.

Surprise is one of the principles of war.

With the Boers concentrating their main effort in the purely local Spion Kop sector, he knew that a relatively swift thrust by the 60th could turn the flank before the enemy could send troops to meet it. With Twin Peaks held, Buller and Warren could use the unemployed regiments to exploit the capture and take Spion Kop from the rear.

The advance was made in two columns: one, on the right, under the 60th's Commanding Officer, Lieutenant Colonel Buchanan-Riddell; the other, on the left, under Major Bewick-Copley. The columns advanced steadily across the open veldt until the Twin Peaks area was reached. Major Bewick-Copley assaulted the left Peak to turn the flank while Colonel Buchanan-Riddell contained the right Peak and repulsed the defensive fire.

At last the classic principles of fire and movement were being used by the British; the 60th carried out their traditional extended order battle drill at its brilliant best. Under heavy fire, Major Bewick-Copley's column stormed the steep defiles that led to the summit, charged the Boer entrenchments with fixed swords (bayonets) under covering fire from Colonel Buchanan-Riddell's column, and drove the defenders into a panic retreat. Finally, both columns occupied the area.

Nearly 100 Riflemen were dead and 70 wounded.

The eagerness for pursuit was understandable but its tactical unsoundness gave General Buller an opportunity to intervene. Further exploitation, without supporting troops or artillery, would have led the rest of this gallant force to disaster. As it was Colonel Buchanan-Riddell, a hero among heroes, stretched his lines too far. He exceeded his orders, which were to capture and hold the Peaks.

When General Buller learnt of Lyttleton's decision, after the 60th had set off for Twin Peaks, he ordered them to return. Anger replaced his phlegmatic imperturbability. It was increased when his order was blandly ignored. But when the objective was secured his second order was obeyed and the Peaks were abandoned.

General Buller has been severely blamed for his intervention, but a dispassionate view must justify it. Lyttleton's initiative and the 60th's brief triumph should not be underestimated. Nevertheless, the decision to attack Twin Peaks without consultation and co-ordination was unsound. The capture of the objective by itself would not have altered the course of the battle. Exploitation in force could have won it.

It can be argued that if Colonel Buchanan-Riddell, who was killed at the moment of his regiment's triumph, had not extended his lines, Buller might have been persuaded to follow another principle of war, that of reinforcing success.

General Lyttleton presumably thought he would; but his attack, hurriedly mounted without consultation, gave Buller no opportunity to co-ordinate the reinforcing. It is probable that he would not have done so anyway. Dash, initiative, risk, and surprise were not his style.

Lyttleton is well supported by some historians who maintain that General Buller's recall order was the result of pique at his Brigade Commander's apparent insubordination. But Buller's military judgment was tactically correct. He was guilty of a strategic inflexibility which prevented any kind of co-operation or swift change of plan – but that was an inherent part of the Battle of Spion Kop.

Those critics who believe that General Buller could and should have reinforced the 60th's success overlook the lack of a grand design for the battle and the vital logistics.

His decision to fight Spion Kop in isolation and his failure to widen his front are a hallmark of his inflexibility. His own immobility was reflected in his dispositions. The static Natal Field Force was unable to move quickly to follow up the kind of success which the 60th had achieved.

Even if this had been possible, Lyttleton's independent decision ignored the logistics of reinforcement. Time is relative, but even a more mobile force than that commanded by General Buller could not have provided reinforcements with supporting artillery in time. When Colonel Buchanan-Riddell had secured Twin Peaks darkness was soon to fall over the veldt.

In theory this was the moment when victory was there to be grasped. Twin Peaks had been captured, the Boer flank attack had failed, and the Boers themselves were emotionally and physically exhausted. Had there been a grand, sweeping strategic plan, this would been the hour of triumph.

Success now depended on Thorneycroft's determination and ability to hold on throughout the night and fight again the following day . . .

The ubiquitous Winston Churchill, who had been buzzing around all day, was impatient for news and aggressive action. Indifferent to the shooting and heavy shelling he clambered to the top of the upper plateau. He was shaken by the devastation. "Corpses," he wrote later "lay here and there. Many of the wounds were of a horrible nature. The splinters and fragments of the shells had torn and mutilated in the most ghastly manner . . . The scenes were among the strangest and most terrible I have ever witnessed . . ."

Realizing that Thorneycroft could not fight another day he rode back to General Warren's headquarters. With characteristic passion and impetuosity he begged Warren's staff not to let Spion Kop become another Majuba Hill. Their apparent indifference angered him, and he was passed on to Warren himself.

Churchill, nominally a subaltern officer but in reality a war correspondent, had no respect for incompetent generals, or indeed for their rank. A depressed, weary Warren was infuriated by the young Churchill's insistence and rudeness: "Who is this man?" he demanded, and ordered him to be arrested.

A very junior officer he may have been, but Winston Spencer Churchill was the son of the redoubtable Randolph, someone with considerable influence in high places . . . and a Marlborough. Warren's attitude changed. If only to be free of him, he sent Churchill back to Thorneycroft with a message. More troops together with the Mountain Battery which had arrived from Frere were to be sent up during the night, and the Sappers were to prepare the ground so that guns could be hauled up next day . . .

Twilight is brief on the African veldt. The shooting and gunfire died down as night fell and brought relief to the British and Boers alike. They had been locked in fatal combat since dawn. Enfiladed, surrounded on three sides, outgunned and out-manoeuvred, Thorneycroft and his soldiers had almost lived up to the military cliché of defending to "the last man and the last round".

Thorneycroft himself was in despair at Warren's lack of support and communication. Winston Churchill had not yet arrived with news of new plans. But Thorneycroft could hear the almost unbearable cries of the dying and wounded. He was distressed by the piles of dead. About 40 per cent of his force were casualties.

We have read Churchill's reference to the horror and the carnage. Two other references are important to a clear understanding of Thorneycroft's conduct. A Boer observer wrote that he saw 60 bodies in one trench, "entangled as if the dying men had clutched each other in their death struggle". Deneys Reitz wrote: "There cannot have been many battlefields where there was such an accumulation of horrors within so small a compass." And that was written after Deneys Reitz had served in World War I.

By their own standards the Boers had also suffered heavy losses, both on the upper plateau and in their flank attack on the lower one. Their failure to dislodge the British troops had lowered their resistance. They had seen the Twin Peaks attack cut short. Another attempt the next day could succeed.

First in small groups, and then in larger numbers, they deserted the crest line until only a thinly-spread outpost remained. Below the crest, horses were harnessed to the laagered wagons. The pony-mounted commandos joined them for a general withdrawal. Only Opperman's and Prinsloo's commandos stayed below the Kop while the others moved off. "We did not know," Deneys Reitz wrote, "the cruel losses that the English had suffered, and we believed they were clearly holding their own."

But Botha did not believe this. He was confident that if the British did stay during the night, they would use the same tactics the next day. He estimated that if they sent fresh troops and got their artillery up the hill, they would have no room for manoeuvre. He did not believe that General Buller would now change his plan and set up a wide, flanking pincer movement.

He acted decisively and stopped the retreat.

Again we can rely on Deneys Reitz for a first-hand impression: "As the foremost wagons moved away, there came the sound of galloping hooves and a man rode into our midst. I could not see his face in the dark but word went round that it was Louis Botha . . . so eloquent was his appeal that in a few minutes the men were filing off into the darkness to re-occupy their positions."

The main body waited below the crest and on nearby high ground, ready for a counter-attack at first light. Louis Botha believed that a sudden, surprise assault could drive the British off the upper plateau. He had won the hearts of his men. Now he must strike swiftly to hold them.

But just before first light four of Prinsloo's men crept over the crest line to recover some of their wounded.

No sentry nor a single voice nor shot

challenged them. There were no sounds except for the moans and cries of the British casualties. The Boers stole slowly further forward.

"To our utter surprise," Deneys Reitz wrote, "we saw two men on the top triumphantly waving their hats and holding their rifles aloft . . . The English were gone and the hill was ours."

Spion Kop had been abandoned. A battle which had been won was lost. It was an emotional as well as a tactical victory for the Boers. An English translation of Spion Kop is Spy Hill, so named by the original *voortrekkers* who saw the promised land of Natal from it.

On the upper plateau the final phase had been a terrible dilemma for the heroic Thorneycroft. By a tragic irony, like the Lancashire Fusiliers he had tried to rally earlier in the battle, he too was the victim of battle fatigue. By 7.00 p.m. his will to fight, let alone to win, had gone.

When Winston Churchill reached the upper plateau with Warren's message, Thorneycroft had made his fateful decision. There is some suggestion of disagreements between him and Colonels Cooke and Crofton, but eventually they were reluctant partners to the withdrawal. Colonel Hill is also reported to have disagreed; but a close study of the last hours makes it certain that Hill was still on the lower plateau where he had been left in charge while Major General Coke had gone to Warren's headquarters. Coke therefore escaped responsibility for the withdrawal, although an earlier message of his to Warren had hinted that this might be a possibility.

General Coke's Brigade Major had made sure that his chief was not involved. After he had heard that Thorneycroft had ordered the retreat he issued a statement at 10.30 p.m.: "This withdrawal is absolutely without the authority of Major General Coke or Sir Charles Warren. The former was called away by the latter shortly before 10.00 p.m. . . . Our men were holding their own. Someone without authority has given orders to withdraw, and has incurred a grave responsibility. Were the General here he would order an instant re-occupation of the Heights."

While we can admire the Brigade Major's loyalty we must doubt his sincerity. He must have known that General Coke had hinted at an earlier withdrawal; and he must have known too that Coke's skulking, irresponsible conduct during the day did not suggest a leader in a crisis.

Poor Thorneycroft was to suffer a terrible retribution for his decision. But his humanity, and perhaps a military instinct that something should be salvaged for another day, can be judged by his remark: "Better six battalions down the hill than a mop up in the morning."

But the fighting spirit of the regimental soldiers was still alive. Despite all they had endured on that truly awful day there were protests as the withdrawal began.

On their way back they passed the lower plateau where Colonel Hill tried to stop them. Thorneycroft, however, insisted that as the formally appointed commander he would not countermand his own orders.

To the end, he was astonished by Warren's ignorance of the situation. General Warren would not accept that the plateau was untenable. While he reported Thorneycroft's failure to General Buller he sent a cavalry patrol forward to cover a re-occupation. This futile gesture was no more than a token. The Boers could have picked them off one by one without leaving their natural fortress. Secure in it, they did not risk a pursuit, and Thorneycroft's troops left the battle area unmolested.

Finally, nothing in this extraordinary battle equalled its bizarre end. General Buller crossed the river, summarily replaced General Warren, and organized a planned co-ordinated withdrawal "in good military order".

"Old fighting Buller" had rescued his troops and restored their faith. They were ready to follow him into the next battle.

6 The Sequel: Responsibilities, Recriminations and Reforms

History has judged Thorneycroft harshly. But like some other unsuccessful generals he was the victim of extraneous circumstances. A soldier with no experience of co-ordinated command, he was probably the wrong choice for such responsibility. Other, more senior, officers might have stayed on the Kop throughout the night. They might have made a counter-attack when the Boers were themselves withdrawing. They might also have stayed and suffered even heavier casualties.

Unquestionably Thorneycroft should not have withdrawn without having consulted General Warren; but his failure to do so was another symptom of bad communications.

Some historians believe that a well-timed night attack by Thorneycroft might have won the battle. This stems from a dubious opinion of a Boer officer who said: "There is no doubt that if the British had attacked that night the Federals would have made a poor resistance at the utmost, and their rout would have been a matter of course."

This ignores two vital factors: the resolution of Botha and, later, of his subordinates; and that the British army were not night fighters. Night operations similar to those of later wars were not common practice in any army. In the chaos in the Kop, with exhausted, baffled troops, any such attack would have failed. It has been argued that Generals Buller and Warren could have made a plan, using the 20,000-odd reserves. But this overlooks that second vital factor . . . the British army were not night fighters by instinct or experience.

Even with trained staff and troops, a night operation is a highly specialized operation. It demands first-class planning, co-operation of all arms, a complex communications system and above all time.

In the end the Battle of Spion Kop was a desperate gamble, and Louis Botha won it.

The British reported 322 killed, 583 wounded, and 300 prisoners. In fact, nearly 1,500 were killed, wounded, and missing. The Boers reported 58 dead, 140 wounded; but at least 150 were killed.

If Thorneycroft had won he would have been a national hero, with perhaps a Victoria Cross to reward his personal courage, and a military career of unbroken progress. As it was, the emotional scars of that battle and the disgrace of his withdrawal haunted him until he died more than 30 years later.

He was an ordinary soldier (with extraordinary courage) who did just what he had to do. Arthur Conan Doyle's comment in *The Great Boer War* was compassionate and realistic: "One finds it difficult to understand why so momentous a decision, upon which the whole operation depended, should have been left to the judgment of one man who in the morning had been a simple Lieutenant Colonel . . ."

The immediate sequel to Spion Kop was scarcely less farcical than the battle itself. Lord Roberts, who was preparing the relief of Kimberley on the western front, advised Buller not to attack the Tugela Heights again until Roberts himself could support him.

Throughout a military career that spanned more than 50 active years, "Bobs" was scarcely ever criticized. But his handling of General Buller showed that even this national hero could be indecisive and vacillating. First, he had left him with too much independence on the Tugela, and this led to the loss of Spion Kop. Now, instead of giving a direct order, he "advised" him not to attack. Buller ignored the advice and was defeated again at Vaal Kranz, a hill to the east of Spion Kop.

This comparatively minor action resembled Spion Kop in that, again, the British captured a summit, were pinned-down by deadly Boer fire and after two days withdrew across the river. Before that, however, Buller had signalled his Commander-in-Chief for even more advice. Roberts suggested, but gave no firm order, that he should press home his attack.

He did relieve Ladysmith, at his fourth attempt on 28 February 1900 . . .

The drama of the inevitable inquest on Spion Kop unfolded slowly.

Immediately after that battle, and before he attacked Vaal Kranz, General Buller sent a preliminary dispatch to London. He made General Warren solely responsible for the withdrawal which, Buller said, he himself discovered "in the morning". The home newspapers reported this, and General Warren became the public scapegoat.

Five days later, General Buller wrote his official dispatch, part of which was marked "not necessarily for publication". In it he said that "Warren seems to me to be a man who can do well what he can do himself but he cannot command, as he can use neither his staff nor his subordinates. I can never employ him again on an independent command . . ."

The entire dispatch was a masterpiece of detachment. It might have been written by an independent observer. Nowhere in it did Buller accept any responsibility.

With an unbelievable disregard for the consequences, the War Office suppressed the "secret" part. Although many people knew the truth, two years were to pass before the secret was revealed . . .

Meanwhile, the more thoughtful soldiers and civilian students of war began to realize that Spion Kop was one of the decisive battles in British military history. It had not affected the balance of power or influenced political actions. But it was to be the heart and core of unprecedented changes in British army organization.

While General Warren was publicly blamed for the defeat, General Buller's career continued at its zenith. This, as much as anything, illustrates the habits of the military hierarchy; and it is a key not only to the Spion Kop disaster but also to the South Africa campaign, which cost some 20,000 lives, more than 100,000 sick and wounded, and £200 million.

General Buller was sent home at the end of 1900, not in disgrace or to a harmless, face-saving posting, but to his former appointment as Commander-in-Chief Aldershot, the Army's most important field command. He was rewarded for his South African service by being made a Knight Grand Cross of the Order of St. Michael and St. George (GCMG).

No one protested at his Aldershot posting; yet Field Marshal Lord Roberts had, at last, criticized him. Commenting on Spion Kop, "Bobs" said: "The chief fault lay in the disinclination of the officer in supreme command to assert his authority and see that what he thought best was done."

Buller also lost the confidence of other senior officers including Generals Lyttleton and Dundonald. Winston Churchill wrote: "He plodded from blunder to blunder and one disaster to another, without losing the regard of his country or the trust of his troops, to whose feeding as well as his own he paid serious attention . . ."

The South African War, with Spion Kop as its centrepiece, unmasked a tight, masonic-like military society and marked the end of the regular officers' mutual protection association. In World War I, unsuitable generals were to be removed, albeit slowly. In World War II, with Winston Churchill's unforgotten eye-witness South African experience, they were to be removed with ruthless speed.

Surprisingly, General Warren – who had returned to England early in 1900 – made no great public complaint against the accusations. Improbably, he was said to be unaware of the report's "secret" parts, but there is some fragmentary, unsubstantiated suggestion that he was among those who forced its release.

Before that, the published version had raised doubts and posed some uncomfortable questions. There was endless speculation in London that the truth had been suppressed. Newspapers openly criticized Buller's handling of the Tugela battles, and Spion Kop in particular. They fed their readers with hints and innuendoes about his poor morale. They highlighted his surrender advice to Sir George White, at Ladysmith. In a sensational attack, *The Times* said he was not suitable to command at Aldershot.

Buller was stung to angry self-defence. After an astonishingly tactless speech, in 1901, he was relieved of the Aldershot command, and put on half pay. He retired to his Devon estate where he died in 1908.

But retirement did not end his personal agony. In 1902, L. S. Amery (later the Right Honourable L. S. Amery, PC, MP), who had been a *Times* correspondent in the War, published the first of his seven-volume *The Times History of the South African War*. His criticisms of Buller's Natal campaign, and of Spion Kop in particular, were scathing. A year later the "secret" part of the dispatch was released. And in 1903, Buller tried, pathetically, to defend his conduct before His Majesty's Commission on the War in South Africa.

Its report was the most devastating attack ever made on the British army. It led to comprehensive and revolutionary organizational changes. It said that the whole military system as it stood at that date (1899) was tested by the War in South Africa, and concluded that with a few exceptions it had failed the test.

The greatest battle of the War, Spion Kop, reflected all of the disasters of the campaign. No other battle provided the Royal Commission with as much evidence.

Paradoxically, there might never have been an inquest if Spion Kop had been won and Ladysmith relieved. The British army would have continued with its exclusive, closed world and would have been totally unprepared for World War I in 1914.

Scarcely any part of the army escaped the devastating indictment. By implication, as well as by direct statement, Viscount Wolseley, as the overall Commander-in-Chief, was the head of the guilty men. His complacency, his philosophy of fighting bygone battles against natives, his select circle of well-chosen, well-disposed subordinates, his intrigues, and his massive indifference to change, had been the major contribution to a badly-won victory.

No one expected the Commander-in-Chief to be personally responsible for the unbelievable errors and shortages exposed by the Royal Commission; but Wolseley's slackness, lack of vision, and poor staff organization, had been the cue for the army as a whole.

Every aspect of the War came under the Commission's microscope, and that included all of the blunders at Spion Kop: the central strategy of the campaign; life and death details that affected the soldiers in the field. The sights of over 2,000 Lee-Enfield rifles were so faulty that there was a firing error of 15 inches to the right at 500 yards. The lines of communication by which an army is maintained and administered had little formal existence. Logistics, the science and arithmetic by which an army is moved, were conspicuously absent; consequently, the forward infantry, cavalry, and artillery were separated from essential supplies, ammunition, equipment and, as at

Spion Kop, artillery. Although the British had been in South Africa for more than half a century, accurate maps, which would have helped Buller and Warren, were unavailable.

A poor water supply system and any lack of water-testing equipment was a prime cause of the high casualty rate from disease. But the Royal Army Medical Corps and the newly-formed Army Service Corps earned high praise for their devotion to duty despite a lack of organized transport, badly-equipped and understaffed hospitals and field dressing stations, insufficient medical supplies and nursing orderlies.

Lord Roberts complained bitterly to the Commission of the casual appointment of staff officers: "Staff officers," he said, "cannot be improvised"; he was equally bitter about the quality of the artillery's guns which he claimed were inferior in range, firing, and accuracy to the Creusot and Krupp ordnance.

The poor standard of officers and other ranks received caustic criticism. The other ranks were the products of bad social conditions and reacted to the poor environment of army life. The army was blamed, perhaps unfairly, for not having attracted a better type of recruit, and of neglecting the education and welfare of the serving soldier who, the Royal Commission said, lacked initiative and resourcefulness and depended too much on his officers.

Both before and since the South African War, soldiers have always depended on their officers, but there was no doubt of the Commission's view of officer training and selection.

After the findings of the Commission, the Royal Military College, Sandhurst, and the Royal Military Academy, Woolwich, were never to be the same again. They were always to send some unsuitable officers to the army, but they overcame the stigma of the Report. This said that the passing-out standards at both Colleges were already low, but there was evidence to show that officer-cadets who "failed to reach even this standard" had nevertheless received their commissions. And of many of those who were commissioned, the Report said: "Keenness among officers is out of fashion . . . and it is not correct form to show it."

The Commission's Report was a masterly analysis. Its proposals and recommendations set an ideal which, inevitably, was never achieved. But when the British Expeditionary Force went to France in 1914, it was better trained, better equipped, and more efficient than any other in the history of the army. For the first time it was supported by a trained General Staff.

The South African War ended on 31 May 1902, with the signing of the Treaty of Vereeniging, after the Boers' defensive strategy had finally failed.

Louis Botha evaded capture. When he visited London, in 1903, he was astonished to receive a hero's welcome. He was asked to call on King Edward VII who invited him to become the first Prime Minister of the Union of South Africa, which office he assumed in 1910. Four years later he fought with characteristic stubbornness to overcome internal opposition when he led the Union into World War I, as Britain's ally.

Appendix 1 – Buller's Order of Battle

2nd Division (Lieutenant General Clery)

under Major General Hildyard:
    2nd Battalion The Queen's Royal Regiment (West Surrey)
    2nd Battalion The Devonshire Regiment
    2nd Battalion The West Yorkshire Regiment (The Prince of Wales's Own)
    2nd Battalion The East Surrey Regiment

under Major General Hart:
    1st Battalion The Royal Iniskilling Fusiliers
    1st Battalion The Border Regiment
    1st Battalion The Connaught Rangers
    2nd Battalion The Dublin Fusiliers

Division supported by 19th, 28th 63rd Batteries Royal Field Artillery; one squadron 13th Royal Hussars; half company The Corps of Royal Engineers.

5th Division (Lieutenant General Sir Charles Warren)

under Major General Lyttleton:
    2nd Battalion The Cameronians (Scottish Rifles)
    3rd Battalion The King's Royal Rifle Corps (the 60th)
    1st Battalion The Durham Light Infantry
    1st Battalion The Rifle Brigade

under Major General Woodgate:
    2nd Battalion The King's Own Royal Regiment (Lancaster)
    2nd Battalion The Lancashire Fusiliers
    1st Battalion The Prince of Wales's Volunteers (South Lancashire)
    1st Battalion The York and Lancaster Regiment

Division supported by 7th, 78th, 73rd Batteries Royal Field Artillery; one squadron 13th Royal Hussars.

Corps Troops (one Brigade under Major General Coke)

    Imperial Light Infantry
    2nd Battalion The Somerset Light Infantry (Prince Albert's)
    2nd Battalion The Dorsetshire Regiment
    2nd Battalion The Middlesex Regiment (Duke of Cambridge's Own)

Corps Troops supported by 61st Howitzer Battery Royal Field Artillery; two 4.7 naval guns; eight 12-pounder naval guns; one squadron 13th Royal Hussars; half company The Corps of Royal Engineers.

Cavalry

1st The Royal Dragoons
14th Royal Hussars
Four squadrons South African Horse
One squadron Imperial Light Horse
Bethune's Mounted Infantry
Thorneycroft's Mounted Infantry
One squadron Natal Carabineers
One squadron Natal Police
One company King's Royal Rifle Corps Mounted Infantry
. . . six machine guns.

Appendix 2 – Boer Forces

All organized in commandos raised from particular districts. The following were among those which took part in Spion Kop battle:

Carolina	Pretoria
Free State	Standerton
Frankfort	Vryheid
Heidelberg	Wynberg

In addition there were General Schalk Burgher's commando (the Staats-Artillerie), and the Transvaal Police (the ZARPS).

Notes for Appendices 1 and 2

It may not be generally known that an Order of Battle does not necessarily signify an order of fighting. In Buller's Order of Battle, for example, the 2nd Division took no real part in the Battle of Spion Kop itself. Of the Boer commandos the Carolina and the Pretoria were the dominant ones at the Kop, but General Schalk Burgher's were the defenders at Twin Peaks.

Appendix 3 – Weapons

British

Artillery: 15-pounder field guns, Royal Field Artillery; 5.7 Howitzers Royal Field Artillery; 4.7 naval guns; 12-pounder naval guns.

Rifles: 0.303 Lee-Metford and 0.303 Lee-Enfield.

Machine Guns: 0.303 Maxims; 1-pounder Hotchkiss.

Boer

Artillery: Mainly 94-pounder French Creusot fortress (or siege) guns; 65 mm German Krupp and Creusot quick-firing field guns.

Rifles: Almost entirely Mauser rapid fire, with clip mechanism.

Supporting Weapons: Mainly Vickers-Maxim guns (known as pom-poms) firing a succession of 1 lb shells containing a small bursting charge.

The Boers also had a miscellaneous assortment of other small arms but these were seldom used.

A Boer picquet at one of the defensive positions which surprised General Woodgate's troops on 23 January 1900 (*Radio Times Hulton Picture Library*).